AF207025

ADDICTED to Gambling

John Allen

ReferencePoint Press®

San Diego, CA

For more information, contact:
ReferencePoint Press, Inc.
PO Box 27779
San Diego, CA 92198
www.ReferencePointPress.com

LIBRARY OF CONGRESS CATALOGING-IN-PUBLICATION DATA

Names: Allen, John, 1957– author.
Title: Addicted to Gambling/by John Allen.
Description: San Diego, CA: ReferencePoint Press, Inc., 2020. | Series: Addicted | Audience: Grade 9 to 12. | Includes bibliographical references and index.
Identifiers: LCCN 2019011569 (print) | LCCN 2019012323 (ebook) | ISBN 9781682825709 (eBook) | ISBN 9781682825693 (hardback)
Subjects: LCSH: Compulsive gambling—Juvenile literature. | Compulsive gambling—Treatment—Juvenile literature.
Classification: LCC RC569.5.G35 (ebook) | LCC RC569.5.G35 A44 2020 (print) | DDC 616.85/841—dc23
LC record available at https://lccn.loc.gov/2019011569

Contents

The Gambling High

Scott Stevens, age fifty-two, pressed the red button on the Triple Stars three-reel slot machine one more time. He had been playing the machine all night and had nearly emptied his dwindling bank account via the ATM. Losing once more, he left the Mountaineer Casino, located outside New Cumberland, West Virginia. It was nearly noon, and he had to write a letter to his wife. In the envelope he also enclosed a check for his last $4,000 and gave her detailed instructions on how to save what was left of the family finances. He wrote how much he loved her and their three precious daughters. "Our family only has a chance if I'm not around to bring us down any further," Stevens wrote. "I'm so sorry that I'm putting you through this."[1] Then he drove to some soccer fields, loaded a 12-gauge shotgun, sat on some railroad ties that lined the parking lot, and ended his life.

An Addiction on Par with Substance Abuse

Individuals like Stevens are addicted to gambling, a condition also called compulsive or problem gambling. This addiction can wreck a person's life. Over a period of ten years, Stevens's gambling habit had resulted in occasional large wins followed by strings of catastrophic losses. In just one year, Stevens suffered more than $4.8 million in losses. His gambling problem led him to max out his credit cards, squander his family's retirement money, and even embezzle funds from work. Once his theft was discovered, he lost his high-paying job and narrowly avoided jail. Yet he continued to hit the casinos, often several times a week. Like millions of problem gamblers in America, Stevens could not resist the lure of the next big score.

Gambling addiction is similar in many ways to substance abuse. The thrill of winning floods the brain's pleasure center with feel-good chemicals, like the rush of a drug high. A compulsive gambler will chase that feeling more and more recklessly, heedless of the money wasted and the damage to his or her personal life. As losses mount, a gambling addict will increase the size of bets in an attempt to get even. All too often the habit will grow into an obsession, causing a person's daily life to spin out of control. Like a drug abuser, the problem gambler develops a tolerance to the euphoric rush of winning. He or she then will seek riskier bets to deliver the same thrill.

Experts note that for most people, occasional gambling is harmless. Trouble starts when a person becomes preoccupied with gambling, when he or she can't wait to get back to the casino, racetrack, or computer screen. Gamblers' thought processes can become distorted, leading them to believe they have a winning system or a lucky charm. They may even blame their losses on a machine. As Canadian psychologist Elizabeth Hartney says, "Problem gamblers sometimes attribute human characteristics to inanimate objects . . . thinking that a particular machine is punishing, rewarding or taunting them."[2]

Gambling Opportunities Abound

Addicted gamblers have more opportunities to feed their habit than ever before. Legalized gambling, once contained to Nevada and Atlantic City, New Jersey, has now spread to most of the United States. In 1988 Congress voted to regulate gaming on Native American tribal lands. This law led to the construction of hundreds of new casinos across the country, many in rural areas, with yearly revenue in the billions. When state-run lotteries are included, nearly every state today features some form of gambling.

Depending on where they live, Americans interested in placing a wager can choose from casino games and slot machines, horse racing, sports betting, online games of chance, scratch cards, and bingo. In 2018 the US Supreme Court ruled that states could offer sports betting on professional and collegiate games, which promises to significantly expand this potentially risky activity. For problem gamblers, the landscape is filled with temptation that is nearly impossible to avoid.

Young people are not immune to gambling's influence. Besides the stress caused by a parent's gambling, teenagers can become hooked on online games themselves. And though almost all legal gambling is age restricted, any teenager with access to

a credit card can register for online gambling. Spending hours on gambling sites while alone in their bedroom, some young people are especially vulnerable to getting hooked. Just one thrilling jackpot can plant a dangerous seed.

Need for Therapy

Like other addictions, problem gambling often requires professional help. "Anyone who is concerned about their gambling might ask 'Can I stop if I want to?'" says Christian Nordqvist of Medical News Today. "If the answer is 'no,' it is important to seek help."[3] Therapists can assess a gambler's personal situation and decide if the problem is related to anxiety, depression, or another mental health issue. Certain medications for substance abuse can be useful treatment for obsessive gambling as well. An addicted gambler might also benefit from a self-help group such as Gamblers Anonymous, in which people share their experiences in trying to kick the habit.

With gambling widely accepted in the United States today, problems with compulsive gambling seem likely to grow. Family members, friends, and physicians should be on the lookout for those with a gambling addiction. Left to themselves, gambling addicts like Scott Stevens can lose not only a string of expensive bets but everything else, including their life.

Chapter One

A Surprisingly Powerful Addiction

Gambling addiction affects a variety of people in the United States, both old and young. Take the case of Stephanie Iacopino, a sixty-five-year-old woman from Toms River, New Jersey. Iacopino became a compulsive gambler who lived for the excitement of playing the machines in dimly lit casinos. At the height of her addiction, Iacopino slipped out one night with an ATM card linked to a church charity on which her husband served as treasurer. She drove to the Borgata casino in Atlantic City, where in short order she drained the account of more than $18,000.

Iacopino soon pleaded guilty to second-degree theft, which carries a possible jail term of five to ten years, and she was ordered to restore the church funds. Following a series of strokes and hospital stays, she served almost four months in a correctional facility for women near Clinton, New Jersey. She then spent nearly two years in the state's intensive supervision program. Today Iacopino is a recovering gambling addict trying to avoid the lure of slot machines. One slip could be disastrous for her and her husband. "We don't have a nest egg," Iacopino admits. "We live paycheck to paycheck."[4]

A Serious Health Disorder

Gambling addiction is a serious health disorder, a fact that many people may find surprising. Gambling can be addictive in much the same way that drugs and alcohol are. It is what mental health experts call a behavioral addiction, and it can take over a person's life. "The concept that problem gambling is not a moral defect but instead a disorder is relatively new," says Howard J. Shaffer, a professor of psychiatry at Harvard Medical School. "Most experts and clinicians now consider gambling addiction as a legitimate biological, cognitive, and behavioral disorder."[5] As Shaffer notes, gambling excessively can also lead to other problems. Iacopino's story shows just how serious these problems can be for a longtime gambling addict.

Gambling is a pastime that goes back centuries. A person who gambles risks something of value—usually money, but other assets as well—in the hopes of getting back something of even greater value. Some games of chance involve skill and strategy, such as playing poker or blackjack. But many types of gambling are based entirely on luck. Addicted gamblers—whether casino regulars, card players, horse race bettors, or even online stock traders—all crave the excitement of risking large sums on the next spin, the next card, the next race. They know the odds are not in their favor. That is why gambling is such a successful industry—the house always wins in the end. Yet addicted gamblers will continue to place larger and larger bets in pursuit of a big jackpot. As losses mount, they will bet all the more recklessly, thinking they can get even if they just keep trying.

This is the hallmark of a behavioral addiction: not being able to stop. Addicted gamblers lose self-control. They cannot keep themselves from placing one more bet. The very thought of quitting can make them anxious or depressed. They are constantly seeking the high of winning without regard for the terrible consequences that can follow. To someone looking on, their actions can appear foolish. But they are in the grip of a powerful force that does not yield to ordinary logic. In fact, losing can actually feed the addicted gambler's excitement by increasing the tension of the next bet.

Some games of chance involve skill and strategy, such as blackjack (pictured). But many types of gambling are based entirely on luck.

Signs of Gambling Addiction

Compulsive gambling has been called the silent addiction. This is because it generally leaves no physical signs. Often the family members and friends of an addicted gambler have no idea there is a problem until disaster strikes. Jodie Nealley, a recovering gambling addict, notes, "Another difference between substance abuse and gambling is that you can't see it. I didn't come home smelling like bourbon. I didn't come home with red eyes or needle marks. I didn't miss work. I didn't have my spouse call me in sick because I was hung over. My addiction—my illness—was invisible and all the more devastating because of that."[6]

Physical signs may be lacking, but there are many behavioral signs that provide clues to a gambling addiction. Gambling addicts often will resort to lying to hide their obsession. When they lie about how much time they are spending at the casino or racetrack, there is obviously a problem. Compulsive gamblers are consumed with thoughts about gambling and are always planning their next session. They are usually desperate for money to feed their habit. They may turn to family, friends, coworkers, or shady loan sharks. Some even steal to get cash quickly. "Living with a gambler in the past, I would frequently have jewelry missing or items of value just disappear," says Sydney Smith, a psychotherapist and gambling counselor. "Later I would learn that my gambler would pawn these items to obtain gambling money or to chase his losses."[7] Sudden credit card debt or the need to take a second mortgage on a home are further signs of trouble.

Gambling addicts often begin to change the ways they interact with other people. They may develop a new circle of friends met through gambling. They often become impatient, irritable, or quarrelsome due to the stress of repeated losses. Their gambling may cause them to miss family events or fail to meet obligations at work. If confronted, they may become angry and deny they have a problem. As addicts sink further into debt, these personality changes will likely grow worse.

Adolescents have their own telltale signs of gambling addiction. For example, a teenager may spend hours on online gambling sites in his or her room, have a sudden drop in grades and unexplained absences from school, show unusual interest in talk about gambling or sports betting, withdraw from friends, and get caught borrowing or stealing money.

Risk Factors by Age and Gender

Gambling addiction is less widespread than alcohol or drug addiction, but it is still a serious problem. According to the North American Foundation for Gambling Addiction Help, about 2.6 percent of the US population has an issue with problem gambling.

That represents almost 10 million Americans who are battling a gambling addiction. Among these are about 750,000 young people aged fourteen to twenty-one. Research shows that 3 percent to 5 percent of those who gamble eventually become addicted to it. There is also a connection between gambling addiction and alcohol abuse. People with disorders related to alcohol use are twenty-three times more likely to develop a gambling problem. Perhaps not surprisingly, as a person's gambling addiction becomes more severe, the person is at an increased likelihood of committing a crime to support or get money for his or her habit.

Those aged twenty to thirty, when the compulsive behavior of youth is combined with more personal freedom, show the greatest risk of becoming addicted to gambling. Young people are more likely to gamble for recreation with friends. They also spend more time gambling online. However, problem gambling is also increasing among older Americans. Loneliness, isolation, boredom, and cognitive problems can all contribute to gambling addiction among seniors.

A recent study of forty-three thousand Americans conducted by the National Epidemiologic Survey on Alcoholism and Related Conditions found gender differences related to gambling addiction. Men are about three times more likely than women to develop a gambling addiction at some point in their lives. They also tend to start gambling at a younger age. Women are more apt to become addicted to gambling in their forties or later. Research shows that women can develop a gambling addiction quite rapidly, often within a year of their first wagers. By contrast, men take an average of four years to become hooked on gambling.

Men and women also differ in the forms of gambling they prefer. Men tend to like games that offer the illusion of skill and control. These include table casino games such as blackjack, dice, and roulette. Women are drawn to slot machines, bingo, and a numbers game called keno. With disposable income for women on the rise and females in control of nearly 80 percent of household

Signs and Symptoms of Compulsive Gambling

The Mayo Clinic regards compulsive gambling as a serious condition akin to drug or alcohol addiction. If not treated, it can wreck the gambler's life and the lives of those around him or her. According to the Mayo Clinic, the signs and symptoms of compulsive gambling include the following:

- Being preoccupied with gambling, such as constantly planning how to get more gambling money
- Needing to gamble with increasing amounts of money to get the same thrill
- Trying to control, cut back, or stop gambling, without success
- Feeling restless or irritable when you try to cut down on gambling
- Gambling to escape problems or relieve feelings of helplessness, guilt, anxiety, or depression
- Trying to get back lost money by gambling more (chasing losses)
- Lying to family members or others to hide the extent of your gambling
- Jeopardizing or losing important relationships, a job, or school or work opportunities because of gambling
- Resorting to theft or fraud to get gambling money
- Asking others to bail you out of financial trouble because you gambled money away

Source: Mayo Clinic, "Compulsive Gambling." www.mayoclinic.org.

spending in the United States, gambling by women—including gambling addiction—seems certain to grow.

Other Risk Factors

Gambling addiction also is linked to certain mental health issues. Psychiatric problems such as depression, anxiety, and obsessive-compulsive behavior are major risk factors for problem gambling.

The House Always Wins

It is the first rule of gambling: The house always wins. That means the casino, racetrack, bingo parlor, lottery commission, or whoever is running the gaming show always makes money. And generally lots of it. Gamblers have winning streaks, and those who have the discipline to quit when they happen to be ahead can leave with some of the house's money. But overall, casinos and other gambling establishments are very successful at separating hapless gamblers from their hard-earned cash. That is how gambling parlors stay in business and make healthy profits. In the end, the house always wins.

Casino games are carefully designed so that the odds are always stacked in the casino's favor. The size of this advantage varies with different games. In roulette the house edge is 5.26 percent. This means for every $1 million wagered at the roulette tables, the casino is likely to make a little more than $50,000. The rest—about $950,000—goes back to the bettors. The house edge in slot machines is much greater, a fat 17 percent. Blackjack tends to be smaller, perhaps only 0.28 percent. Addicted gamblers know the odds are against them in all these games. Yet they still play for hours, convinced they can double their winnings or get back what they have lost. The longer they pump money into the machines, the more the law of averages comes into play. As too many addicted gamblers learn ruefully: The house always wins.

People with bipolar disorder are known to engage in risky behavior, such as placing wild bets, when undergoing a manic episode. Individuals with manic tendencies are also prone to seek the excitement of gambling. Those who suffer from depression often use gambling to distract from emotional pain. Military veterans suffering from post-traumatic stress disorder show increased risk for gambling addiction. Studies show that 8 percent of veterans display symptoms of gambling problems and 2 percent develop full-blown gambling addiction.

Certain personality traits can make a person vulnerable to developing a gambling addiction. A major risk factor is impulsive behavior. Lack of impulse control leads a gambling addict to keep hitting the play button on a slot machine or place a reckless wager on a long shot at the racetrack. "It should be noted that impulsiveness and compulsiveness are different types of behavior," states the mental health site Recovery Ranch. "Compulsions are generally habitual in nature, characterized by actions that are repetitive or ritualistic. Impulsive behaviors, on the other hand, tend to be goal directed or pleasure/sensation seeking; pleasure is derived from the act."[8]

Gambling addicts also often lack coping strategies to remain calm and logical in stressful situations. They look for patterns in unrelated events like separate rolls of the dice and believe they can win big by capturing a hot streak. They may also exhibit antisocial behavior, denying there is a problem and refusing to listen to those who offer help. A family history of gambling problems or substance abuse is another major risk factor for gambling addicts.

As opportunities for gambling expand around the country, so do the risk factors for gambling addiction. The National Council on Problem Gambling (NCPG) notes that gambling in the United States generates revenue of more than $115 billion for federal, state, and local governments. Yet gambling also incurs $6.5 billion in social costs, including law enforcement and health care expenses related to problem gambling. These costs often seem invisible, but they reflect the misery that gambling addiction can cause. For example, the recent Supreme Court decision that legalized sports gambling for all fifty states has the potential to create many new gambling addicts of all ages. "Everyone who profits from sports betting bears responsibility for gambling problems," warns Keith Whyte, NCPG executive director. "The only ethical and economical way to maximize benefits from sports betting is to minimize problem gambling harm."[9]

From Addiction to Financial Disaster

With gambling more widespread than ever, the problems associated with gambling addiction threaten to wreck families, businesses, and friendships. They can even result in suicide. One of the main consequences of gambling addiction is financial disaster. What begins as a pleasant pastime, with the loss of a few dollars here and there, can spiral down rapidly into financial ruin. When gambling addicts scramble to make back their losses, they usually dig themselves into a deeper hole. Soon every waking hour is devoted to worries about money. Financial risk can lead to reckless borrowing, debt problems, maxed-out credit cards, mortgage foreclosures, and bankruptcy.

Money problems creep up as a person's gambling habit grows worse. Mary, who lives in Minnesota, started gambling as a way to escape stress. But she soon found herself hooked. "I was on autopilot," she says. "I had no ability to stop. I couldn't limit the time or the money I was spending on gambling."[10] She began to visit the casino three or four times each week. The large cash advances she took from her credit cards left her with bills she could not pay.

Mary managed to take a break from gambling for several months, only to clean out her bank account the first time she returned to the slot machines. She took money from work that she had no means to repay. Yet she continued to deny that her life was in a shambles. "I didn't want to admit I was a compulsive gambler," Mary says. "I didn't want to say it out loud. It's hard to admit you're a liar and a cheat and a thief."[11] Luckily for Mary, her employer helped her get treatment for her addiction instead of pressing charges. Mary is today a recovering gambling addict who is rebuilding her finances and committed to staying clean. Many compulsive gamblers are not so fortunate when faced with financial ruin.

Consequences at Home and Work

Gambling addiction brings many more negative consequences both at home and at work. When a gambling addict is caught lying about his or her habit, the family loses trust in the individual.

Adolescents have their own signs of gambling addiction. For example, teenagers may spend hours on online gambling sites in their bedrooms, hiding their addiction from their parents.

This leads to incredible stress and tension in the household. Children lose their sense of security and begin to worry about the future. Money problems, constant deception, late nights away with no phone calls, violent arguments, and even domestic abuse can cause family ties to fray to the breaking point.

The spouse of a gambling addict faces special pressures. A wife or husband often experiences anxiety and feelings of helplessness as the problem spirals out of control. He or she may lose self-esteem or get tangled in deceit by trying to make excuses for the gambler's behavior. The constant struggle to hold things together and provide emotional support for the children can be exhausting. After months or years of trying to cope, a spouse may decide the only way out is divorce. Many families are torn apart by gambling addiction in this way. A woman who belongs to Gam-Anon, a support group for family members of problem gamblers, recalls how her husband's secret gambling habit nearly destroyed their lives.

I watched him go from a loving, compassionate husband and father to a shell of a person who couldn't even function enough to go to work each day, she says. He became a habitual sneak and liar. . . . My children and I had no respect for him. I wasn't sure which one of us would have the nervous breakdown first.[12]

Work-related consequences are also severe. Addicted gamblers are more likely to take sick days or leave work early to indulge their habit. They are apt to take advantage of business trips to gamble. Their obsessive thoughts about gambling—and gambling losses—can result in reduced productivity and errors in their work. Relations between a stressed-out gambler and coworkers are often strained. Addicted gamblers with access to company funds face huge temptations to embezzle in order to make up losses. Companies that fall prey to a gambler's embezzlement scheme can suffer damage to their reputation. Ultimately, the gambling addict can lose his or her job and have difficulty finding another.

A Problem Poised to Grow

Gambling addiction is a serious problem in the United States. As more states have legalized various forms of gambling, the risk of addiction has increased. Gambling addiction is not limited to those in the prime of life but actually affects young people and seniors as well. The consequences of compulsive gambling can include marital problems, family disruptions, work-related failures, and financial ruin. This health disorder, if not diagnosed and treated, can wreck not only the life of a gambler but also the lives of his or her loved ones.

Chapter Two

Why Gambling Is Addictive

Deborah Greenslit will never forget the day her problems with gambling began. It was her daughter's twenty-first birthday, and Greenslit was in a lighthearted mood. She accompanied a friend to Mohegan Sun, a resort casino in Uncasville, Connecticut. The pair headed straight for the slot machines. Greenslit, who had gambled some in the past, bet a grand total of $36. Her last pull of the lever produced a stunning jackpot: $752,000. At once Greenslit told herself she now could afford that beach cottage in Maine she had dreamed about for so long.

Two years later, however, her plans had been dashed. She kept reliving that rush of excitement when the slot machine had erupted in flashing lights and ringing bells. Time and again she returned to the machines at Mohegan Sun, hoping for a repeat performance. Instead she gave back all her winnings and much more. Greenslit ended up broke and painfully aware that she was a gambling addict. Ironically, she had worked for years as a therapist and wellness expert, helping people overcome problems with anxiety, personal growth, and addiction. "I was paying attention to everyone else's leaks in life," Greenslit admits, "and I ended up with a gaping hole [in my own]."[13]

Various Signs of Addiction

Gambling offers the tempting thrill of taking a chance and winning against the odds. Most people can gamble occasionally with no ill effects. But for some people the activity holds a powerful attraction that can damage their lives. "The addictive lure is believing that if you just play long enough you will win," says Greenslit. "Often that will happen, but usually not until you have already put in 10 times more than what you won. Then you go for the chase to win your money back, only to dig yourself in deeper and deeper."[14]

Gambling addiction takes hold of a person in several ways. One way is purely physiological. Like addiction to drugs or alcohol, excessive gambling affects the chemistry of the brain in a fundamental way. In 2013 the American Psychiatric Association acknowledged the truth about gambling addiction. That year the group updated its *Diagnostic and Statistical Manual of Mental Disorders* to include pathological gambling as an addictive disorder akin to substance abuse. It is currently the only behavioral disorder labeled as an addiction. This has changed the way people approach gambling addiction and opened new avenues for treatment.

Gambling also has powerful psychological and emotional effects. The addict can fall into a routine just as an alcoholic can crave a drink at a certain time of day. The atmosphere of a casino or sports betting center may trigger the urge to make a wager. Addicted gamblers may win just enough to keep them chasing the big score. Gambling can become an emotional release from tension or stress, one that only causes more stress in the end. And even family members and close friends may not recognize when addiction has taken hold. "A gambling addict is not as easy to spot as a substance abuser," notes Eliot Applegate, a high-stakes poker player who has encountered many problem gamblers. "Drug addicts display obvious physical signs of withdrawal, such as altered appearance and behavior (i.e., red eyes and twitching). But a gambling addict can go to work and spend time with their families as usual."[15] Often it is only when financial disaster strikes that an addicted gambler's condition becomes known.

For most gambling addicts, the obsession grows over a period of months or years. But some can become hooked quite suddenly by a thrilling win. They may discover in themselves a surprising appetite for risk and even recklessness. And like substance abusers raising their dosage, gambling addicts may find themselves needing to increase the risk to get the same feeling of excitement. This is how gambling addiction can feed on itself and lead to problems with money, work, school, marriage, family, and friends.

Changing the Brain's Chemistry

Too much gambling can actually rewire the brain. This physiological change is one reason gambling is so powerfully addictive. Experts in neuroscience and genetics have demonstrated how this change in brain chemistry closely resembles the effects of substance abuse. A gambling addict becomes hooked on wagering much like a drug addict becomes hooked on meth or heroin.

The change occurs in the brain's reward system, a series of circuits located in the middle of the cranium. The reward sys-

Like addiction to drugs or alcohol, excessive gambling affects the chemistry of the brain. It creates a physiological reaction that can drive some people to chronically need more.

tem links several regions of the brain that govern movement, memory, pleasure, and motivation. Activities that promote health or well-being, such as eating a delicious meal or having sex, activate neurons in the reward system. The neurons produce a chemical called dopamine, which is a neurotransmitter or chemical messenger. Dopamine makes a person feel pleasure and satisfaction. And, as the Oaks at La Paloma treatment center's website on addiction explains, "Dopamine does more than make us feel wonderful; it helps us learn what makes us feel that way."[16] Winning even a modest jackpot produces a flood of dopamine in the gambler's brain just like taking a drug would. The euphoria when dopamine levels spike is unforgettable, leading the gambler to chase that feeling again and again.

In fact, it is not only winning that stimulates dopamine neurons. Research shows that the risk and uncertainty of gambling also produce a rush of excitement. The breathless anticipation gambling addicts feel with each wager or play helps feed their addiction. Even losing can raise dopamine levels in addicted gamblers. Experts believe this is why addicted gamblers tend to chase their losses even when their reckless bets seem illogical.

Gambling addicts tend to have a dopamine imbalance. Their brain produces more of the chemical than the typical brain does. Their addiction grows from repeatedly experiencing the rush from dopamine. Addicted gamblers also lack impulse control and cannot stop themselves from seeking this rush of excitement and pleasure. Over time the brain adapts by producing less dopamine and responding less to its effects. Like drug abusers, gambling addicts can develop a resistance to the dopamine rush. "I became numb. Insensitive," says Stephen, an addicted gambler. "I wasn't even excited when I was winning anymore, the value of a dollar was gone."[17] When that happens, gamblers like Stephen must make increasingly risky bets to experience the same thrill as before. Ten-dollar bets become five-hundred-dollar bets, and total losses can skyrocket.

Weakened Links for Impulse Control

Excessive gambling seems to weaken the connections in the brain that help control impulses. Scientists have found that neural pathways that link the reward system to the prefrontal cortex (located above and behind the eyes) grow weaker with repeated gambling. Since the prefrontal cortex aids in impulse control, addicted gamblers find it more difficult to walk away from a slot machine or roulette wheel. This is how the addiction reinforces itself. According to Anne Lingford-Hughes, coauthor of a UK study on neuroscience and problem gambling, "The frontal lobe can help control impulsivity, therefore a weak link may contribute to people being unable to stop gambling, and ignoring the negative consequences of their actions. The connections may also be affected by mood—and be further weakened by stress, which may be why gambling addicts relapse during difficult periods in their life."[18]

Outside factors may play a part in weakening impulse control. For example, some prescription drugs increase the risk of impulsive behavior and problem gambling. Among these are dopamine agonists, which are used to treat Parkinson's disease and can cause a person to lose impulse control.

Withdrawal symptoms also can affect the problem gambler's impulse control. Problem gamblers trying to quit are more likely to relapse due to withdrawal symptoms. These symptoms are similar to what drug abusers experience, although not as physically taxing. Withdrawal is caused by a sudden lack of dopamine

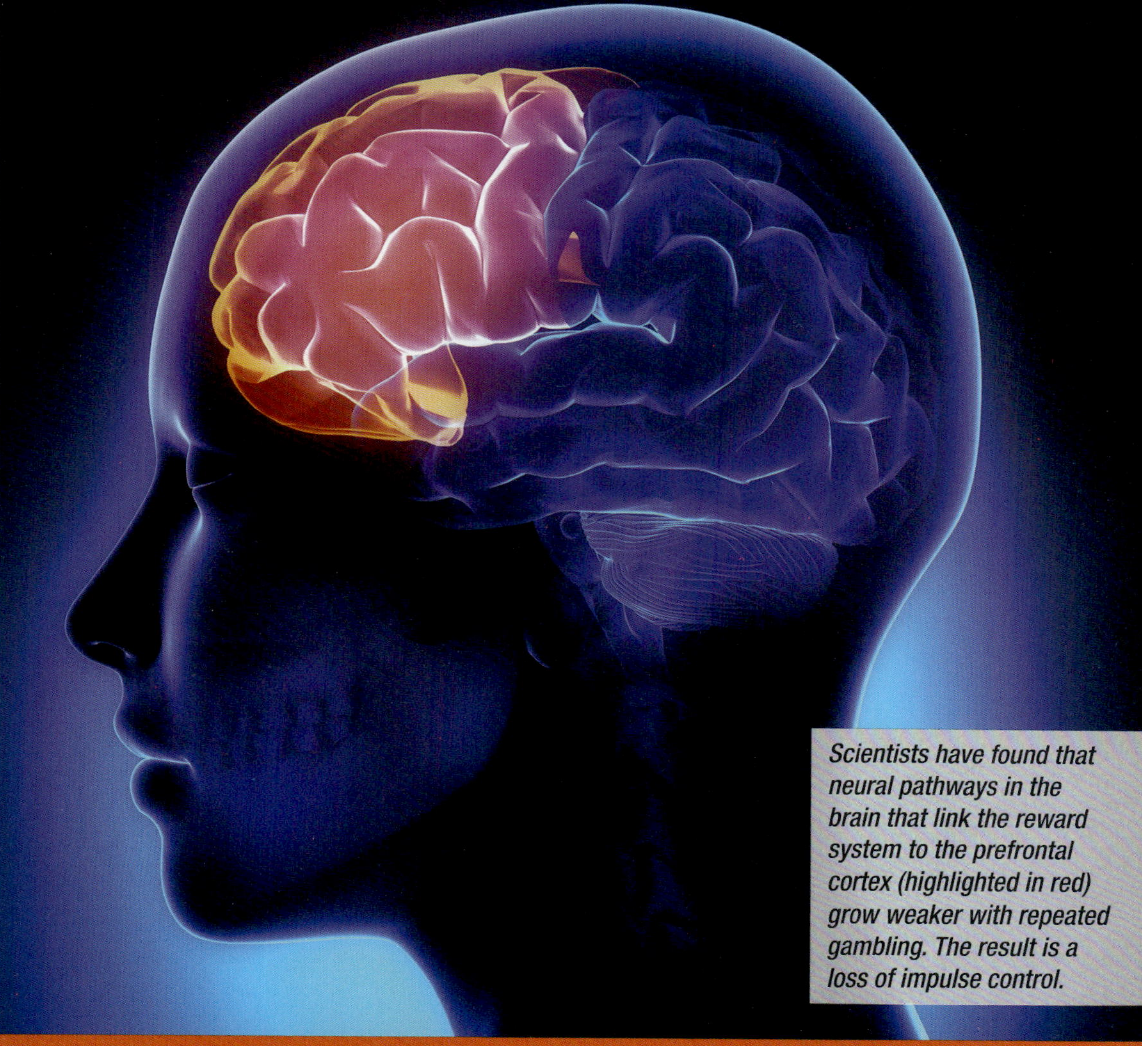

stimulus. The gambler's brain tries to rewire itself back into a normal state. Symptoms can be both physical and emotional. Gambling addicts who try to kick the habit can suffer from insomnia, nausea, headaches, depression, and weight gain or weight loss. They may feel irritable, restless, and anxious, with a strong urge to return to the casino or online game. Therapy is often required to help the gambling addict manage the stress of quitting.

The Psychology of Partial Reinforcement

Some factors that lead to gambling addiction are psychological. As shown in psychological studies, rewards affect how people

Drugs That Can Lead to Compulsive Gambling

Ann Klinestiver, a West Virginia high school teacher, received a drug called Requip to control the tremors she experienced from her Parkinson's disease. The drug cured her tremors but soon revealed a powerful side effect. Klinestiver, who had no history of gambling, suddenly grew obsessed with playing slot machines. She found herself spending up to eighteen hours at a time at the casino. Over several years she gambled away her entire life savings, more than $250,000, and lost her husband to divorce. Suspecting Requip had affected her behavior, Klinestiver's doctor took her off the drug. Within a week her gambling compulsion vanished.

Parkinson's sufferers like Klinestiver lose massive numbers of dopamine neurons in the back of the brain. Requip and similar drugs, called dopamine agonists, are designed to increase the amount of dopamine in the brain. However, the higher levels of dopamine can lead to compulsive behavior, including cravings for gambling, food, drugs, and sex. A 2014 study in the *Journal of American Medicine* found that patients who used dopamine agonists were 277 times more likely to develop problems with impulse control than users of other prescription drugs. Researchers estimate that 10 percent to 15 percent of patients may develop problems with gambling addiction. According to Thomas Moore, an expert on drug safety, "The FDA [US Food and Drug Administration] should place more prominent, clear warnings on these drugs, and individuals who take these drugs need to be monitored by physicians and caregivers."

Quoted in Joseph Stromberg, "Warning: This Parkinson's Drug Can Make You Addicted to Gambling, Sex, or Food," *Vox*, January 15, 2016. www.vox.com.

behave and how they learn. Gambling is a perfect example of this. Whether through online poker, blackjack, slot machines, or scratch cards, gamblers need occasional rewards to maintain their interest and keep them playing. Through all their losses, they retain a strong memory of their last win. This convinces them to keep placing bets. As long as they continue to win occasionally, they will not give up or quit playing.

Psychologists call this partial reinforcement. Addicted gamblers are conditioned by occasional wins to risk increasing amounts of their money in hopes of an even bigger score. In the worst cases they may keep playing until all their money is gone. As the well-known psychologist B.F. Skinner once noted, "If the gambling establishment cannot persuade a patron to turn over money with no return, it may achieve the same effect by returning part of the patron's money on a . . . schedule [of partial reinforcement]."[19]

Partial reinforcement plays out every day at casinos. A player begins by risking a few dollars on a slot machine. The machine does not pay out on the first few plays, and the person becomes ready to quit. Then the next push of the button produces a small win. The person regains interest and actually puts more money into the machine. A half hour later the player's money is almost gone, but a larger win, this time accompanied by lights and bells, leads to even more money going into the machine. At the end of the evening, the player likely will have lost far more than he or she ever intended to spend. In this way an addicted gambler can blow through large amounts of money with ease.

A related psychological hook is what is known as the near miss effect. Near misses include the online poker hand that is one card away from a winning straight flush, the gaming machine with one reel just short of lining up for a jackpot, and the lottery ticket that is one number away from a winner. The lure of having apparently come so close to winning is powerful. "Gamblers experiencing the near miss of an almost winning hand, spin, or lottery ticket take it as a sign that they should keep playing," says Jamie Madigan, a psychologist and expert on video games. "And they often do. . . . This is irrational given the presumably random chance involved, but we are not wholly rational beings."[20]

The Gambler's Fallacy

Another psychological factor in gambling addiction is also irrational. The so-called gambler's fallacy is the idea that the outcome of a game of chance is somehow affected by previous outcomes. This can lead gamblers to believe that a string of losses means that a big win is almost certainly on the way.

The gambler's fallacy seems sensible, but it goes against the laws of probability. Gamblers can get caught up in a game of chance and look for patterns in the outcomes of a roulette wheel spin or a roll of the dice. But in reality, each spin or roll is an independent event, with no connection to the one before it or the one after. The odds of hitting a certain number remain the same for each play. Suppose a poker player has a 25 percent chance of winning a hand. After four or five unsuccessful hands, she may think the odds indicate a win is due. However, that 25 percent chance applies only to the hand she is currently playing. The odds have not improved—in fact, they have no relation to the hands she has previously played.

To take another example: A gambler might keep an eye on a slot machine that has failed to pay out for the previous few plays. By falling for the gambler's fallacy, he might reason that a large jackpot is bound to be in store. As a result, he gets on the machine and proceeds to bet increasingly large amounts. But the idea of finding a pattern in the payouts is an illusion—it is not grounded in math. That is how the addicted gambler can convince himself to double his bets despite huge losses. He will tell himself he is overdue for a winning streak, as his money disappears.

Illusion of Control and Loss Aversion

Another common psychological pitfall for addicted gamblers is known as the illusion of control. Many are prone to think their success at games of chance is due to skill or savvy, not random luck. This irrational belief can lead them to make foolish wagers. For instance, research shows that people have more confidence in

choosing their own lottery numbers than in taking machine-picked numbers. Gamblers often bet more in a dice game when they get to throw the dice themselves. Some throw the dice a bit harder to "get a larger number." The illusion of control also prompts a gambling addict to look for complicated reasons why a certain playing strategy met with success. A slot machine player might press the button harder, try to make the reels stop on command, and talk to the machine to get the desired result. Roulette players will make swift calculations on their smartphones that have nothing to do with actual probability. Even casinos sometimes yield to the illusion of control. Blackjack dealers have been known to lose their jobs if too many players are winning at their tables.

The Monte Carlo Fallacy

The gambler's fallacy is also called the Monte Carlo fallacy. The latter name comes from a famous incident that occurred in Le Grande Casino at Monte Carlo on August 18, 1913. Monte Carlo, a resort still known for its beaches and gambling parlors, is located in the principality of Monaco on the southeastern coast of France. On the night in question, the players around the roulette wheel at Le Grande Casino witnessed an astounding run. The little white ball landed on the color black twenty-nine times in a row. The probability of this happening has been calculated as 1 in 136,823,184.

As the streak reached ten in a row, players began to double their bets. They assumed, via the gambler's fallacy, that the next spin of the wheel was bound to produce the color red. The recklessly high wagers continued for nineteen more turns of the wheel—in fact, they continued to grow. By the time the streak came to an end, the casino had raked in the equivalent of two million dollars and left most of the bettors with empty pockets and a woeful story to tell.

The players in Monte Carlo forgot that each spin is a separate event. The odds of each one coming up black that night were still only eighteen out of thirty-seven—a little less than 50 percent. (The wheel included thirty-six numbers plus a slot for zero.) It was an expensive lesson in the gambler's fallacy.

Addicted gamblers also fall prey to loss aversion. Repeated losses lead to frustration and anger. Gamblers feel the need to place another bet quickly to erase a large loss. They lose sight of how unlikely it is that this strategy will succeed. As losses mount, addicted gamblers will keep on placing bets. They are no longer drawn by the excitement of winning but merely hope to regain their lost money. Chasing losses, as this behavior is called, is one of the clearest indications of a gambling addiction.

Emotional Factors

For many addicted players, gambling is an escape from negative or upsetting emotions. They may gamble to relieve stress, anxiety, boredom, loneliness, and/or depression. Someone caught in a troubled marriage may turn to gambling as a welcome distraction. Seniors are especially prone to use gambling as emotional support. They begin by seeking the companionship of friends at a casino or bingo parlor. Once gambling becomes a habit, however, it can turn into an obsession with lots of unhealthy consequences. The addicted gambler often stops thinking logically and gives way to emotional responses. He or she may become angry or defiant in the attempt to win back losses.

Gambling addiction has physiological, psychological, and emotional causes. Physically, it can resemble substance abuse in the way it rewires the brain to pursue the dopamine rush of winning. Psychologically, the addiction is reinforced by occasional jackpots that eventually are gambled away. Gambling addicts may fall prey to muddled thinking like gambler's fallacy or the illusion of control. Emotionally, addicts can abandon logic in their attempts to recover their losses. Overall, gambling addicts court personal disaster and financial ruin. As psychologist Elizabeth Hartney notes, "Gambling is an ineffective and unreliable way of acquiring money. For someone to become addicted to gambling, their . . . thought processes must become distorted to the point where this central truth eludes them."[21]

Chapter Three

How Does Someone Become Addicted to Gambling?

The seeds of gambling addiction can be planted early in life. Writing on the recovery website Lanie's Hope, one young man describes an annual Christmas fair at his elementary school. He was only six when he discovered a game of chance for a quarter a play. He would bounce a ball onto a board of colored squares. If he picked the right color where the ball landed, he would win a prize. He spent the rest of the day running from room to room begging his relatives for quarters. As the young man recalls:

> Already I understood it wasn't the fact that losing meant money was lost that mattered, but that you were out of the action, if the quarters were gone. The crazy thing is from that day forward quarters, dollars, credit cards, or anything else of value only had one purpose; they were a tool to gain that high I got for the first time that day of my first Christmas Fair. I came home that night and could not sleep and I lied in bed with so much energy and a warm feeling like a heat flash: one would of thought my parents gave me speed. Every year other kids at school thought of Santa Claus when December came around, but to me I knew that the ball and that feeling that felt so good was here again.[22]

More Gambling Opportunities than Ever

Like the young man and his Christmas fair, many addicted gamblers start with an exciting experience, a sudden win or unlikely jackpot, that stays with them. And today there are more opportunities to begin gambling than ever before. Every state has some form of legalized gambling. The United States has more than 1,500 casinos, the most of any country in the world. Oklahoma, a small state in terms of its population, now has more than 134 casinos in operation, second only to Nevada in overall numbers. Moreover, casino gambling is only one environment in which to place bets. Americans also can resort to racetrack betting, online gambling, sports betting, card games, bingo, keno, lotteries, and raffles. Never before have there been so many opportunities to become addicted to gambling. "We've made it so legal, so social," says Michael Burke, a recovering gambling addict who spent three years in prison for embezzlement related to his gambling. "We use it to raise money in your churches. You're helping your community if you gamble [in a lottery], because the money is going to schools. But for the person who suffers from addictions: Stay away from it."[23]

Gambling once was mostly a shared activity, but that has also changed. Gamblers today can pursue the activity in secluded corners of large casinos or even online in the privacy of their homes. Even young people can engage in online gaming or sports betting without their parents' knowledge. This anonymity, away from the disapproving eyes of family or friends, can fuel a gambling addiction.

The Initial Thrill of Winning

Many gambling addictions begin when the person wins a large amount early on. The initial thrill of winning often will lead a person to recapture that feeling. The way to do that is to gamble again and again. Jodie Nealley fell prey to this kind of seductive early success. She was already a compulsive person but seemed to have fought through her addictions. In her twenties she had kicked a three-pack-a-day cigarette habit. In her late thirties she had overcome problems with heavy drinking. Gambling's allure, however, proved harder for her to escape.

Thirteen years after her last drink, Nealley attended a business conference at a casino. In between meetings, she drifted to the slot machines. As Nealley recalls, "What happened then was, as any compulsive gambler in recovery will tell you, the worst thing that could have happened for me. I won! . . . Stress, anxiety and a desire to escape all played into this moment when the obsession with gambling took over my life. The slots were my drug of choice so to speak and I loved everything about them."[24]

As Nealley admits, she had a natural tolerance for gambling. She needed more risk to get the same thrill. Betting a quarter at a time left her cold. Even dollar slots lacked excitement. Soon she was playing $100 machines, with maximum bets of $200 a play. She craved the high of making reckless bets. In six months of obsessive gambling, she lost hundreds of thousands of dollars. She tore through her home equity, maxed out credit cards, and borrowed money wherever she could. She gave way to the classic symptoms of gambling addicts: distorted thinking and the illusion of control. "I firmly believed I would win back the money I had lost. I firmly believed that if I kept playing the same machine, even though I had put in thousands of dollars, it would hit big. And when I ran out of legitimate sources of money and began to steal from my employer . . . I truly believed I would pay it back."[25] It took a conviction for larceny and a two-year prison sentence to finally set Nealley on the road to recovery. Her gambling addiction, fueled by that initial rush of excitement, had caused her to lose almost everything

Getting into the Zone

For some gambling addicts, the lure of winning money is beside the point. Social gaming, such as card games or crowded roulette tables, are not for them. What they seek is an escape from their everyday lives, what they call "being in the zone." These gamblers are drawn to slot machines or online games because they can be played alone for hours at a time. Gambling is a way to shut out the world by focusing exclusively on an electronic terminal or smartphone. The thought of gambling by themselves is enormously comforting. In the zone, they find that nothing else matters.

Natasha Dow Schüll, an associate professor of anthropology at the Massachusetts Institute of Technology, spent years studying slot machine players in Las Vegas, Nevada. She discovered that the repetitive rhythm of playing the electronic machines would send players into a trancelike state. Once in this zone, players would forget marital problems, work troubles, social ties, and the responsibilities of daily life. They would often ignore bodily needs.

Researchers discovered that the repetitive rhythm of playing slot machines sent players into a trancelike state. Once in this zone, addicted players escape their troubles and worries.

All that mattered was continuing to play as long as possible. Winning was important mainly because it added to their stake. It allowed these gamblers to keep on pressing the play button or pulling the lever, as if they were machines themselves. Generally, the trance would end only when the money ran out. Mollie, a hotel worker, told Schüll she would play video poker obsessively, squandering her paychecks in binges that sometimes lasted two days. She was not playing to win so much as playing to stay in the zone, where nothing else seemed to matter. To illustrate the extent to which gambling machine addicts like Mollie crave staying in the zone, consider that they sometimes get irritated when a jackpot occurs: They are impatient at the time it takes for the machine to tally the winnings before the flow of play can resume.

Many of the addicted gamblers Schüll has interviewed are aware of the grip that high-tech gambling machines have on them. For them, the world of the casino is displacing the real world. "I could say that for me the machine is a lover, a friend, a date," says one woman, "but really it's none of those things; it's a vacuum cleaner that sucks the life out of me, and sucks me out of life."[26]

Young people addicted to online gambling also seek to enter this zone. They spend hours alone in their bedroom, staring at a computer screen or smartphone display, comfortable in their gambling cocoon. In fact, gambling addiction is similar in some ways to the obsession with social media and the Internet. Children and teens who begin gambling online are also at greater risk of addiction because they lack impulse control. It is estimated that more than 750,000 young people in the United States ages fourteen to twenty-one are addicted to gambling. This number is likely to grow as online gambling sites proliferate and more young people fall under the habit-forming spell of daily play.

Gateway Games

Certain online games, while not strictly gambling sites themselves, can lead to addicted gambling. They are like gateway drugs to a stronger addiction. These games, such as *Candy Crush Saga*,

Fruit Ninja, and *Clash of Clans*, are particularly appealing to preteens and teenagers. For example, *Candy Crush Saga* is a simple game that players access by downloading a free app. The object is to match brightly colored sweets to score points. In its first six years, the app generated nearly 3 billion downloads. Worldwide, users number in the hundreds of millions. Continuously updated, the game offers a dedicated player more than three thousand levels to conquer.

Like early success in gambling, *Candy Crush Saga* offers easy levels at the beginning that hook players with a sense of accomplishment. Each further level that a player passes adds to the satisfaction—and the dopamine rush that leads to addiction. Players are soon conditioned to seek more success through hours and hours of play. As the levels get progressively more difficult, losses begin to outnumber wins, just as a slot machine pays off only intermittently. Like many gambling machines, *Candy Crush Saga* is a game of chance that seems to depend on skill. And it is always as close as a person's smartphone.

Experts say games like *Candy Crush Saga* may lead young people to hard-core gaming sites like online poker or blackjack. Features like the spinning wheel in *Candy Crush Saga*, which offers a player extra moves or other benefits, can entice young players with the excitement of gambling. According to Mark Griffiths, director of the International Gaming Research Unit at Nottingham Trent University in the United Kingdom, "If there is a simulated roulette wheel in a game like Candy Crush, those games should be for adults only, because of the research showing that simulated games are a risk factor for problem gambling."[27]

Increase in Reckless Behavior

As gambling addiction takes hold, individuals begin to act recklessly. They will neglect to keep close account of wins or losses. Mentally they will magnify wins and downplay losses, no matter how large. Often gambling addicts will chase losses with reck-

Temptation for the Addicted Gambler

For individuals battling a gambling addiction, everyday life in America presents lots of temptations. A casual visit to a casino can earn them a loyalty card that offers discounts, complimentary drinks or meals, or a small amount of money for free play. The card, swiped in a slot machine before each session, monitors the gamblers' activity for future offers. Soon the casino knows a great deal about the cardholders: how much they bet, how much they win or lose, how long they play at one machine, and even what time of day they arrive.

Gambling frenzy is hard to avoid. When news reports trumpet a $1.6 billion lottery jackpot, ordinary citizens cannot help chattering about it. What is harmless amusement for most people, however, looms as a hazard for someone with a problem. All that talk about buying tickets to play Mega Millions tempts addicted gamblers to take the plunge themselves. "It can be similar to a drinking problem on New Year's Eve. There's a lot of potential triggers," says Keith Whyte, executive director of the NCPG. "It's a really bad idea to try to gamble more to try to gain back what you've lost, but that's a problem we see—chasing what you've lost." Whyte says when nationwide lotteries like Mega Millions are in the news, calls to gambling addiction hotlines spike by 25 percent.

Quoted in Elizabeth Chuck, "For Compulsive Gamblers, Mega Millions Frenzy Means 'Constant Reminders to Play,'" NBC News, October 22, 2018. www.nbcnews.com.

less bets for the sheer thrill of the risk. After a long night of losing, gamblers will shrug and tell themselves they do not have a problem. At home, they might hide ATM slips from the casino that attest to this recklessness. Some gambling addicts will seek out other avenues for risk, such as sports betting or online stock trading. Friends and family members are likely to notice mood swings from an addicted gambler brooding on the last visit to the casino or sports betting parlor.

Having a great deal of money and free time to spend it can lead to even more reckless gambling. Plenty of sports stars and celebrities become hooked on the thrill of making massive bets.

Charles Barkley, a retired pro basketball player and now a popular TV commentator, claims to have lost millions in his gambling career. "It's a stupid, bad habit. I have a problem," says Barkley. "I went to Vegas a bunch of times and won a million dollars. Probably 10 times. But I've also went to Vegas and lost a million probably three times as much."[28] David Milch, an Emmy Award–winning producer in Hollywood, gambled away more than $25 million at the racetrack. With his fortune gone, Milch was restricted to only $40 a week in spending money, paid out by his wife.

Hooking the Problem Gambler

Casinos play on the psychology of problem gamblers, especially those who play the machines. This is a business decision, since slot machines bring in 40 percent to 60 percent of casino revenue on average. Strategies to keep players pushing the buttons and cranking the levers help keep the profits high. They also contribute to gambling addiction. As one gambling industry consultant told Schüll, "The key [to machine gaming] is duration of play. I

The Addictive Near Miss

Slot machine players regularly find themselves wincing at the one reel that refuses to tick forward into a winning alignment. Makers of electronic gaming machines rely on these near misses to keep addicted gamblers hitting the play button. Programmers design each machine's payout schedule by arranging various possible outcomes on a set of virtual reels. They tilt the odds to make sure that certain outcomes are much more likely to occur. One of these favored outcomes is the near miss, in which a single reel comes close to lining up with the others and delivering a jackpot.

Near misses affect areas of the brain linked to winning, says Mike Robinson, assistant professor of psychology at Wesleyan University. This can increase the urge to keep playing, particularly for addicted gamblers. "Near misses are more arousing than losses—despite being more frustrating and significantly less pleasant than missing by a longshot," says Robinson. "But crucially, almost winning triggers a more substantial urge to play than even winning itself. . . . The size of the dopamine response to a near-miss in fact correlates with the severity of an individual's gambling addiction." As a result, addicted gamblers will continue to play despite the frustration—and often double down on their next bets. This response helps feed a gambling addiction and keeps profits flowing to the casino.

Mike Robinson, "Designed to Deceive: How Gambling Distorts Reality and Hooks Your Brain," Conversation, August 13, 2018. theconversation.com.

want to keep you there as long as humanly possible—that's what makes you lose."[29]

Most casinos do not have clocks or windows. This helps keep players in a state in which the outside world is forgotten and only the present moment matters. Gambling machines are carefully programmed to tantalize players with occasional wins and near misses. Some machines include stop buttons that give players a false sense of control over each spin. Instead of the old three-reel models, many electronic gaming machines now have five or more reels, thus enabling gamblers to make as many as twenty bets per spin. Having more reels also increases the chance for a small win with each play. Time and again a gambler will push the button for a one-dollar play and win forty, thirty, or ten cents in return. This feeds the illusion that the gambler is winning—complete with lights and bells—even though his or her bankroll is dwindling. Occasionally, the machine serves up a larger win to make things interesting. However, the odds are with the house, and many players cannot stop themselves before their money is gone.

Machines also are aimed at producing a trancelike state that industry insiders call "continuous gaming productivity." The electronic displays include flashing lights and musical jingles to create an artificial environment. Bright colors and vivid graphics contribute to the hypnotic effect. Addicted gamblers fall into the machine's rhythm of play, scarcely caring about wins and losses. "The manufacturers know these machines are addictive and do their best to make them addictive so they can make more money," says Terry Noffsinger, an attorney who has brought suit against casinos for contributing to gambling addiction. "This isn't negligence. It's intentional."[30]

Many Routes to Addicted Gambling

People become addicted to gambling in many ways. Often an initial thrilling jackpot will hook someone prone to a gambling addiction. Others may find themselves settling into a comfortable zone of obsessive gambling. As the addiction takes hold, many problem gamblers become increasingly reckless in their behavior. Casinos and gambling machines are designed to take advantage of a gambler's psychology and encourage longer sessions. And the longer addicted gamblers play, the more likely they are to lose large amounts of money.

Chapter Four

A Gambling Addict's Daily Struggle

The law profession might seem like an odd breeding ground for gambling addiction. Yet Delaware attorney Jeffrey Wasserman combined a successful law practice with a compulsive gambling habit for decades. His addiction led him to blow through hundreds of thousands of dollars and all his retirement savings. It eventually wrecked his legal career. When things finally came to a head, with his personal and professional life in shambles, Wasserman laid out three options for himself, much as he would have for a client. He could end his life, take a plane out of the country, or face his addiction and seek help. Wasserman chose the third option. "I raised the white flag in my own mind," he says. "I knew that it was D-day."[31]

Daily Struggles of Gambling Addiction

Today Wasserman, age sixty-three, is three years into his recovery program from gambling addiction. He also serves as development director at the Delaware Council on Gambling Problems. He often speaks to law groups and other business organizations about the struggles of an addicted gambler. Through his outreach to other professionals, he hopes to help them avoid his own crisis.

Wasserman knows firsthand how addicted gamblers must battle their urges on a daily basis. Their struggles may go unnoticed by family, friends, and coworkers for years. As debts and bills continue to pile up, addicted gamblers often refuse to admit they have a problem. They tell themselves they could stop if they really wanted to, but they always have an excuse to go on gambling. As another former gambler observes,

> There are brief moments where they let their walls down and admit to a close friend that they are in trouble. The friend listens intently but has no immediate solution. The next time they see one another, nothing is mentioned and the friend assumes you have it under control. In reality you do not. You go back into your fantasy world and continue to gamble.[32]

When addicted gamblers miss a child's birthday party or some other family event, they blame circumstances beyond their control. They may start to feel sorry for themselves and wonder why their luck is so bad. They may fly off into emotional outbursts that startle those around them. Just when things seem hopeless, a big night at the casino can provide a momentary sense of optimism. Maybe things are not so bad, they think. Then they double down on their bets, convinced they can somehow win back their losses. And the whole self-destructive pattern will repeat itself.

Gambling to Relieve Stress

Many gambling addicts turn to gaming to relieve personal stress from work or family life. This is especially true for people whose jobs create a constant sense of mental strain or uncertainty. As an attorney, Wasserman faced a great deal of stress every day in handling clients' issues. "When lawyers don't develop effective stress management skills, they turn to stress relievers that can lead to addiction," says Wasserman. "One of those stress relievers is gambling."[33]

However, for Wasserman gambling soon became the disease, not the cure. With his ability to set his own schedule, Wasserman could drop by the casino whenever he pleased. Out-of-town visits to clients turned into gambling junkets. Late hours at the office became another excuse to stop off on the way home and gamble. The impulse to try his luck at the casino began to poison everything

he touched. His excitement at winning a case or rescuing a client was transferred to the slot machine and roulette wheel.

Mounting losses from obsessive gambling caused additional stress. Wasserman began to chase losses by gambling even more and making riskier bets. This is the vicious cycle into which many gambling addicts fall. Suddenly, Wasserman could find no relief from stress in any area of his life. His ego as a successful attorney only made the situation worse. Adept at solving his clients' problems, he thought he could avoid the pitfalls of gambling.

Wasserman convinced himself he could outsmart the system and reverse his losses. "If you're an attorney and you gamble in an activity where there's some skill involved, your ego feels that you can win," says Wasserman. "You think you're smarter and wiser and can manipulate the system better." His ego also led him to discount the possibility of becoming addicted to gambling. "Despite all evidence to the contrary, I thought I could stop whenever I wanted," he recalls. "Then I told myself I just didn't want to stop. Of course it was my ego that prevented me from reaching the proper conclusion."[34]

All along, the stress of hiding his problem was added to the strain of financial losses. With his lawyer's ability to argue on his own behalf, Wasserman tried to convince coworkers and family members he was fine. And then came the final reckoning—and his lifesaving decision to get help.

Gambling to Escape Loneliness

Just as some people gamble to escape stress, others gamble to relieve feelings of loneliness and boredom. And this can lead to a habit that spirals out of control. What seem like harmless losses at first can mount into financial pressures capable of turning a person's life upside down. A good example is T.C., a middle-aged former nurse who is divorced and prone to bouts of loneliness. She would go to the casino with her mother and friends to escape being depressed on bad weather days. Once inside, they would scatter and then regroup later to discuss how their luck was running. At the start T.C. would allot herself only twenty dollars for gambling. Over the course of twenty years, that amount steadily grew until she was cashing large checks, returning to the ATM machine for hundreds of dollars a night, and even maxing out credit cards.

T.C. could no longer trust her own judgment. She repeatedly broke promises to herself to curb her spending on the slot machines. She would vow to leave after three hours and end up playing for nearly twelve. If she had some success, she usually continued to play until her winnings were gone. "On the way home, I beat myself up emotionally because my behavior was insane and out of control," says T.C. "After all, I am a smart and frugal person. And I don't lose as much as others. I would wake up in the morning planning my next visit to the casino. Next time, I would do better at controlling my gambling, but I never could control it."[35]

T.C.'s obsessive gambling took over her life. Her self-esteem drained away. Everyday pleasures were replaced by trips to the casino. Her savings account disappeared, and she plunged further into debt. Her efforts to escape depression only left her more miserable. As T.C. observes:

> I didn't lose my house or steal from others, I stole from myself. Money that could have paid off the mortgage or helped grandchildren through college. The gambling winnings were supposed to do that. But it never happened. . . . I began to feel desperate and depressed. With shame, despair began to settle on me. I realized that my gambling was as big a problem as alcohol or drug addiction, and that I needed help.[36]

T.C. received help for three years at Harbor Hall, a treatment center in Petoskey, Michigan. Addiction counselor Paula Musilek has listened to stories like T.C.'s time and again at the center. One woman had served prison time for embezzling more than $17,000 to pay gambling debts. Another patient brought in evidence of his gambling addiction in the form of ten jumbo garbage bags stuffed with scratch-off lottery tickets he had bought. Most regret the misery they have inflicted on others. "[Gambling addicts] cost their families or their business, home, career, school, or use their kids' college funds," says Musilek. "It ripples down to their family."[37]

Impact on Family Members

In addition to its impact on work and finances, gambling addiction can take a heavy toll on families. Dealing with a compulsive gambler raises the stress level of every family member. It often leads to secretiveness, arguments, and hurt feelings that are hard to overcome.

Some gambling addicts turn to gaming to relieve stress from work. This is especially true for people whose jobs create a constant sense of mental strain or uncertainty.

Sometimes, the truth about a spouse's gambling emerges accidentally. One Minnesota woman had always enjoyed gambling with her husband on vacation trips. However, she had no idea he had developed a gambling problem. One day she loaned her husband money to fix his father's car heater. A couple of weeks later, when she saw her father-in-law, she asked him how his car was doing. His puzzled response let her know the story about the car heater was a lie. That was when she began to notice how much time her husband was spending at the casino. Three weeks did not go by without a lengthy session at the slot machines. Sometimes he would squander his entire paycheck on gambling. On those occasions, he was too ashamed to face her and slept over at his father's house. When he finally returned home, he would express remorse and promise never to do it again. But she knew his gambling habit was out of control.

She persuaded her husband to attend Gamblers Anonymous, but he stopped after only a couple of meetings. Her own meetings

A Lot of Wasted Money and Time

Tala knows she has to work hard to regain her husband's trust. When he went to buy a car at a dealership recently, he was turned down because of a low credit rating. He discovered that a credit card he had asked Tala to close out had instead been used to rack up more than $24,000 in debt from casino gambling. Furious, he accused Tala of wrecking his good name. He had never been turned down for a loan in his life.

Tala and her husband are trying to save their marriage in spite of her gambling addiction. She began gambling casually on occasional nights out with him and her extended family. When her husband started working long hours, she took the money he gave her and played slots, roulette, and baccarat (a card game). One night she lost $4,000. "Until then, I never thought I had a gambling problem," says Tala. "But, the truth is, I was lying, hiding things. . . . With every loss I became more desperate to win my money back because my husband had no idea how much money I was losing."

Eventually, Tala could not tear herself away from the casino to pick up her daughter at school. She would gamble for forty-eight hours straight with no food or sleep. She ended up losing more than $100,000 and nearly wrecking her marriage. "I wasted a lot of money," she says, "but I also wasted a lot of time I would have had with my children."

Quoted in Responsible Gambling Council, "Tala's Story." www.responsiblegambling.org.

at Gam-Anon opened her eyes to the problem. She learned how she was actually enabling his gambling by loaning him sums of money to replace his losses. When she refused his next request for cash, he flew into a rage and flung his wedding ring out the car window. When his fits of anger grew worse, his wife had had enough. The couple separated, and she eventually filed for divorce. Despite admitting the extent of his addiction, he refused to stick with a rehab program. He made trips to stay with his brother, supposedly to avoid gambling, but she learned he spent most of his time at the casino. She despaired of ever changing him. As she admits,

It's very difficult being the spouse of a person with a gambling problem. You're afraid to leave your husband for a weekend to spend time with your girlfriends. That's no way to live. I could not live in crisis day in and day out, always knowing there was a little calm before the storm, having to hide my money and never knowing if what he said was the truth or a lie.[38]

Courting Financial Disaster

For many addicted gamblers, the financial consequence of their gambling is like quicksand pulling them steadily down toward ruin. They scramble to keep the extent of their losses hidden from others. The need to make back their losses becomes a daily obsession with no end in sight. Usually, addicted gamblers will grow increasingly reckless in their attempts to somehow save themselves. They cling to the hope that the next big win will turn things around. They continue to bet when the odds are heavily against them and plow small winnings back into a card game, roulette table, or slot machine. This behavior can lead them to drain savings accounts and college funds, borrow recklessly, embezzle money from work, and resort to outright theft. The downward spiral gets a little worse each day. Their health declines and they may have thoughts of suicide. As one British gambling addict put it, "I have thought many times to end my life but found I couldn't do it because of my family I leave behind. . . . Roulette has nearly wiped me off this world."[39]

Embezzlement and Prison

As losses skyrocket, many gambling addicts face the temptation to tap into their employers' funds for a quick fix. Thirty-three-year-old Frederick Boone Price had a high-paying accounting job at a real estate company in Oklahoma City, Oklahoma. In one year he obtained more than 150 illegal cash advances on his company credit card, mostly to finance his gambling habit at local casinos. The amount grew to nearly $400,000. Price tried to hide the transactions by changing the company books, but an outside accounting firm discovered his embezzlement. Sentenced to nineteen months in federal prison, Price also must pay back the stolen money. Having squandered the trust of his employer, clients, and friends, Price resolved to change his

Addicted to Online Stock Trading

Gambling is not limited to casinos, racetracks, or Internet gaming. Some people indulge their taste for risk in online stock trading. The lure of making large amounts of money while sitting in front of a computer screen or holding a smartphone is powerful. Moreover, the idea of being one's own boss and abandoning the nine-to-five grind holds great appeal. Yet trading stocks can be as addictive as playing slot machines at a casino. It affects the brain's pleasure center the same way other kinds of gambling do.

It can also be dangerous to have too much success trading stocks on one's first try. For example, in the technology stock bubble of the early 2000s, many amateur traders assumed it was their own skill that led to big gains. Yet most of these traders were wiped out when the bubble burst and tech stocks plummeted in value. An added danger of trading stocks is the ability to leverage one's account—that is, borrow money to buy more shares. With leverage, moves in the stock market are magnified. And, as economic reporter Brian J. Bloch notes, "The stats show that 90% of amateurs lose pretty consistently. The fundamental problem is that this is a risky, speculative business, and the leveraging goes downward just as fast and as much as it goes upward. If it goes sour on you, you can lose your proverbial shirt and a whole lot more."

Brian J. Bloch, "The Downward Spiral of Trading Addiction," Investopedia, February 22, 2018. www .investopedia.com.

life. "It's not the gambling or the money that's going to make me happy," Price told the judge with tears in his eyes. "I know what's important now."[40]

Some addicted gamblers manage to conceal their embezzlement schemes for years before finally getting caught. Chad Hartzler had a six-figure job at one of the largest farm cooperatives in Iowa. The stress of his work led him to gamble on sports for relief. Often he would lay bets totaling more than $20,000 in a day. When he found he could not cover his losses, he made some off-the-books deals with a client to pay his debts. He offered discounts on seed and chemicals and some free products in exchange for payments in cash. "Using the trust I earned with my co-workers, I was able to cover my tracks for nearly seven years," says Hartzler. However, as he admits, "I wasn't in handcuffs yet, but I was handcuffed by my addiction."[41] When his embezzlement scheme finally was discovered, he ended up accepting a plea agreement that included fifty-one months in federal prison. On his first night in lockup, he cried himself to sleep.

A Legacy of Wrecked Lives

Addicted gamblers face daily struggles with issues of stress, boredom, loneliness, and financial pressure. Their addiction can wreck their lives and leave them desperate to make up their losses and hide their true condition. Their gambling can also damage the lives of spouses, children, family members, friends, and coworkers. At its worst, gambling addiction can lead to embezzlement, jail time, and even suicide. It creates a vicious cycle of lost money and reckless attempts to win it back, a cycle that is difficult to overcome. The best solution is to admit one has a problem and seek professional help.

Chapter Five

Overcoming a Gambling Addiction

Kirby was a longtime addicted gambler living in North Dakota. On too many nights he would wake up in a panic. He would realize that once again he had lost the money needed to pay his bills at the casino. He would wonder how he was going to pay for groceries or to fill up his car to drive to work. Finally he had to acknowledge how far he had fallen, how little control he had over his gambling habit. Taking stock of his life, Kirby made the decision to seek treatment and join Gamblers Anonymous (GA), a twelve-step program for people who desire to stop gambling.

Immediately, his life began to change. He received support from others who knew exactly what he was going through. He found encouragement to forgive himself for past failures and focus on the future. "Today things are much better," Kirby says.

> I feel grateful, calm and more content. . . . It's not that I expect life to be perfect, but taking a day at a time is the key for me. My rent is paid, I have groceries in my home, and gas in my car. . . . I think back of where I was, and how far I've come, and what I want out of life. And I just remember: "Today I am not going to gamble."[42]

Acknowledging the Problem

Experts say a major key to overcoming a gambling addiction is to admit there is a problem, as Kirby did. Too often, gambling addiction is not regarded as a serious problem until it is too late. More than 80 percent of those who suffer from compulsive gambling never seek treatment, despite the devastating effects on their lives and the lives of those around them. "Most people don't realize that problem gambling is a real disorder, just like alcohol or drug addiction," says Sheila Moran, director of communications and marketing at First Choice Services, a nonprofit agency in West Virginia devoted to mental health issues. "They think it's just a bad habit that can be easily ended. The good news is that we find most people who get treatment are able to successfully stop gambling."[43]

Convincing a problem gambler that he or she needs help may be a challenge for loved ones or friends. There are online resources to begin the process of evaluating the problem. For example, the Gam-Anon website offers informal assessment tools for addicted gambling. It directs family members and friends to answer questions such as "Are you worried about the emotional health and/or financial security of a loved one who is gambling?"[44] The website for the National Center for Responsible Gaming offers a Brief Biosocial Gambling Screen to identify gambling disorders. One of the screening questions asks, "During the past 12 months, have you become restless, irritable or anxious when trying to stop/cut down on gambling?"[45]

In some cases, the addicted gambler will initiate the process by confiding in someone he or she trusts. It may be a staunch friend or supportive family member. As addiction therapist Liz Karter explains:

Unlike other addictions, such as with drugs or alcohol, there are no immediate physical signs that an individual may be suffering. Because of this, it is an addiction that is easily hidden and your confidant may have not picked up on your problem. Instead, the indications will have been subtler—you may have started withdrawing from social interactions, been exhibiting mood swings or been unenthused by previously enjoyable activities.[46]

Seeking Professional Help

Once addicted gamblers recognize their problem, the next step is to consult with their primary care doctor. They might also go to a mental health professional for advice. A doctor generally will ask questions about the person's gambling, such as how often the person gambles and the effects on his or her life. Mental health experts stress that an addicted gambler need not gamble every

Gambling addicts can get help in group therapy. Many find the therapy gives them the support and encouragement they need to forgive themselves and look to a more positive future.

day. The key question is whether the person's gambling causes problems, such as emotional outbursts, reckless behavior, depression, or financial troubles. The doctor will also want to review the person's medical history, including drugs and medications that might trigger the gambling impulse. Often the doctor will ask permission to speak with the person's spouse, family members, or friends. The goal is to find the extent of the addiction and whether others are aware of it. Confidentiality laws require the patient to give permission for this line of questioning.

The addicted gambler may also receive a psychiatric assessment from a therapist. He or she might answer questions about the signs and symptoms of his addiction. The therapist will want details about the gambler's thoughts, feelings, and behavior patterns that accompany the urge to gamble. The patient likely would be evaluated for other mental disorders related to his or her condition. These include substance abuse issues, stress, anxiety, attention-deficit/hyperactivity disorder, and bipolar disorder. Above all, the addicted gambler learns that breaking the habit and reclaiming an orderly life calls for hard work, tough decisions, and constant discipline.

Treatment for a Gambling Addiction

For the hard-core addicted gambler, checking into a rehabilitation center may be the best option. There individuals can focus on their problem without distractions. Some addicted gamblers may resist pressure from a spouse, friend, or employer to take such a drastic step. After all, gambling is a socially accepted and legal activity, with endless commercials touting its pleasures. However, what is relatively harmless for some people can be deadly for others. Spending time in a treatment center may be the best way for an addicted gambler to regain control of his or her life. Getting treatment on an outpatient basis is more common, but for some it may not go far enough. Intensive treatment helps the addict resist his or her urge to gamble and also provides a

Funds for Treating Gambling Addiction

In the United States the gambling industry is investing huge sums in new casinos and sports betting sites each year. Despite the fact that such investments are bound to produce more problem gamblers, little money is made available for addiction treatment.

It is not hard to see why these needs are mostly ignored. Even though experts have shown that gambling addiction is rooted in a chemical imbalance in the brain, many people still consider it a moral and personal failure. As a result, treatment for addicted gamblers continues to be shortchanged. About 5.4 million Americans suffer from gambling addiction, yet fully 20 percent of US states provide no funds to treat this ailment. Although 2016 saw $24.4 billion in state and federal funds spent on treatment for drug and alcohol addiction, less than $75 million went toward gambling addiction.

Keith Whyte, executive director of the NCPG, hopes to change that imbalance. Whyte is lobbying Congress and state legislatures to divert more money to treatment for problem gamblers. The NCPG is also pushing for more consumer protections for online sports gambling, such as strict rules against underage gambling. Whyte is hopeful that change is on the way, but he knows it may be a struggle. "Right now problem gamblers are a little bit out of sight out of mind," he says, "and some state legislators seem to want to keep it that way."

Quoted in Dustin Gouker, "National Council on Problem Gambling: States Have Done 'Poorly' on Building Sports Betting Laws," Legal Sports Report, March 4, 2019. www.legalsportsreport.com.

chance to repair fractured relationships and bring some order to family finances. Taking this important step shows a commitment to change.

Treatment for addicted gambling is much like that for other addictions, such as alcohol and substance abuse. Many individuals receive treatment as an outpatient. This means continuing to live at home while attending classes and counseling sessions about gambling addiction. Outpatient recovery allows a person the freedom to work or go to school like normal, but it also increases the opportunity to gamble. The person can join a twelve-step program like GA, enroll in one-on-one therapy sessions, and learn how to make lifestyle changes. Above all, the addicted gambler must swear off all gambling. Even playing the lottery or betting on a football game could trigger a relapse.

One effective method for treating addicted gamblers is called cognitive behavioral therapy (CBT). This talk-based therapy seeks to change gamblers' behavior by altering the way they think, feel, and understand themselves and the surrounding world. CBT identifies a person's harmful or irrational attitudes—such as craving risk or believing in lucky streaks—and conditions him or her to replace them with a more positive, rational, and constructive outlook.

In CBT an addicted gambler works one-on-one with a therapist to complete activities designed to reinforce healthier attitudes and responses. "CBT particularly explores the conflicts between what we want to do and what we actually do," says psychologist

Once addicted gamblers recognize their problem, the next step is to consult with their primary care doctor. The doctor can evaluate their physical and mental health, and recommend the next steps the gambler might need to become healthy again.

Elizabeth Hartney. "And while people with addictions may regret these [negative] behaviors, it can be hard to stop repeating them, sometimes without the person really knowing why."[47] In CBT addicted gamblers are taught to identify what triggers their gambling, unlearn those behaviors, and set up rewards for themselves for not gambling. When successful, CBT can create lifesaving changes in an addicted gambler's overall attitude and behavior patterns.

The Twelve-Step Approach

Addicted gamblers in recovery can also seek help in support groups such as GA. Founded in 1957, GA is a twelve-step program for people who have severe problems with compulsive gambling. GA's only requirement for membership is a commitment to stop gambling. More than one thousand GA groups have been formed in the United States, with many more located worldwide. Although GA members are predominately male, more females have joined in recent years.

In its twelve-step approach, GA resembles Alcoholics Anonymous and other substance-abuse and behavioral programs. A twelve-step program consists of a set of steps to guide individuals who wish to overcome addiction and behavioral problems. GA members are each assigned a sponsor to help them follow the steps in order. Each step is more rigorous than the last, leading the individuals to stay focused on their commitment to change. Subjects attend regular meetings with other members in which they discuss their progress on the twelve steps. For example, GA's first step has the individual acknowledge the problem: "We admitted we were powerless over gambling—that our lives had become unmanageable." The twelfth step encourages members to share their success with others: "Having made an effort to practice these principles in all our affairs, we tried to carry this message to other compulsive gamblers."[48]

> "We admitted we were powerless over gambling—that our lives had become unmanageable."[48]
>
> —The first step in the GA twelve-step program

The Danger of Relapse

Like other recovering addicts, problem gamblers always face the danger of relapse. One recovering gambler has blogged about how he made the mistake of going to a racetrack for a friend's birthday. The results were disastrous, since he lost $23,000 in one day—half of his life savings. Nine months of abstaining from gambling and attending GA meetings seemed wasted.

Actually, however, experts in addiction therapy say relapses are not uncommon. Addicted gamblers may encounter an unexpected trigger or succumb to gambling for stress relief. Although a relapse is alarming to family members and friends—especially when they are skeptical to begin with—most often such behavior represents only a temporary setback. It should be regarded as serious but not grounds for despair. Only if the relapse continues is the gambler's recovery in question.

Much can be determined by how the person reacts to a relapse. Someone who is committed to changing his or her life will show genuine remorse for upsetting loved ones and breaking promises. The best way to show support for someone struggling to kick a gambling addiction is to work through a relapse with the person, looking for reasons why it occurred and planning how to avoid temptations in the future. "A gambling addiction relapse is not a failure verdict," says Rick Benson, a certified gambling counselor. "Rather, relapse can be a brutal but essential learning point for some people recovering from gambling addiction."

Rick Benson, "Dealing with Gambling Addiction Relapses," Algamus Gambling, March 28, 2018. www.algamus.org.

Many addicted gamblers find comfort in discussing their problems at GA meetings. The idea that listeners know exactly what they are going through gives them strength to continue. Casey is an addicted gambler who would binge at casinos, occasionally losing thousands of dollars in one night. She laughs at her own irrational thinking, driving miles to avoid a tiny ATM bank fee during the day but shrugging off a 10 percent casino fee for cash advances when in the middle of a gambling spree. She is hopeful that GA will change her disordered life. As Casey admits, "I have come to the realization that it is impossible to beat this addiction on my own. I have started going to GA meetings, but have not really connected with someone I feel can support me all the way through to the end of my recovery journey. But for now, it's helpful and hopeful to hear success stories at the meetings, hear other gamblers' struggles and know that I am not alone."[49]

There are also support groups such as Gam-Anon that help spouses, family members, and friends who are dealing with an addicted gambler. Gam-Anon is a twelve-step program that provides support for those whose emotional health or financial security is jeopardized by a loved one's gambling.

Following Through with Self-Help Initiatives

An addicted gambler often feels nagging guilt toward those he or she has let down. To show the resolve to change, gamblers can follow through on therapy and support-group progress with their own initiatives. One of the most important things to do is to address financial obligations. Years of reckless gambling can leave a person's finances in chaos. Recovering gamblers should make a personal list of all their debts in detail. These should include money borrowed from friends and family members, credit card balances, missed or overdue payments, and money owed to casinos or gambling websites. In the worst cases, gamblers may have to deal with a home that is lost or in the process of foreclosure. Cars or boats may have been repossessed due to missed payments. The family may have declared bankruptcy to try to attain a clean slate. Making this financial inventory is painful, but it is essential to starting a new life free from gambling.

Another important step for recovering gamblers is to take inventory of all the ways gambling has affected them, their

Years of reckless gambling can leave a person's finances in chaos. In the worst cases, gamblers may lose their homes to foreclosure.

family, and friends. This requires a candid assessment of past behavior. Individuals will be sobered to confront how many lies they have told, how often they have hidden their gambling behavior, how much their health has declined, how fragile they have become emotionally, and how they have wrecked longtime relationships with friends and coworkers. It also helps for them to list all the reasons they gambled, from the feelings of exhilaration at winning to the need to escape boredom and stress at the casino.

In the end recovering gamblers must eliminate all traces of their former gambling life. This includes casino cards, gaming websites, and gambling advertisements. They should avoid friends who still urge them to gamble. It might be necessary to cancel all ATM and credit cards or at least put them in a spouse's name.

Struggling free from gambling addiction is a lifelong project. Nonetheless, even a tiny show of progress can be joyous for the recovering addict. As one young man describes his situation on a recovery website: "I am really trying to tackle this problem seriously this time. My friends have heard it all before but they were very supportive and that made me feel happy as well."[50]

Addicted gamblers have to remember that the urge will always be there inside them, waiting to come out if they succumb to temptation or triggers. It is a long, hard road to recovery but one that can end in a better life for the gambler and his or her family.

Introduction: The Gambling High

1. Quoted in John Rosengren, "How Casinos Enable Gambling Addicts," *Atlantic*, December 2016. www.theatlantic.com.
2. Elizabeth Hartney, "Signs of Pathological Gambling and Gambling Addiction," Verywell Mind, July 1, 2018. www.verywellmind.com.
3. Christian Nordqvist, "What's to Know About Gambling Addiction," Medical News Today, June 19, 2018. www.medicalnewstoday.com.

Chapter One: A Surprisingly Powerful Addiction

4. Quoted in Tanya Mohn, "Fighting Compulsive Gambling Among Women," *New York Times*, April 28, 2017. www.nytimes.com.
5. Howard J. Shaffer, "When Gambling Might Be a Problem," Harvard Health, February 1, 2018. www.health.harvard.edu.
6. Jodie Nealley, "Compulsive Gambling Is an Illness to Which I Lost Nearly Everything. Nearly," BASIS, March 13, 2015. www.basisonline.org.
7. Sydney Smith, "Spotting a Gambling Problem: How Families Can Identify the Main Signs," *Addiction Blog*, February 26, 2017. https://gambling.addictionblog.org.
8. "Habit Reversal for Impulse-Control Disorders," Recovery Ranch, November 15, 2017. www.recoveryranch.com.
9. Quoted in National Council on Problem Gambling, "National Council on Problem Gambling Statement on Supreme Court Ruling on *Murphy v. NCAA*," May 14, 2018. www.ncpgambling.org.
10. Quoted in Northstar Problem Gambling Alliance, "Mary's Story." http://northstarproblemgambling.org.

11. Quoted in Northstar Problem Gambling Alliance, "Mary's Story."

12. Quoted in Gam-Anon, "Personal Experiences." https://gam-anon.org.

Chapter Two: Why Gambling Is Addictive

13. Quoted in Bella English, "Jackpot Fueled Therapist's Gambling Addiction," *Boston Globe*, July 15, 2012. www.bostonglobe.com.

14. Quoted in English, "Jackpot Fueled Therapist's Gambling Addiction."

15. Eliot Applegate, "How the Brain Gets Addicted to Gambling," CoolCat Casino, January 7, 2019. www.coolcat-casino.com.

16. Oaks at La Paloma, "Gambling Addiction and the Connection to Substance Abuse," 2009. www.theoakstreatment.com.

17. Quoted in Gambling Therapy, "Compulsive Gambler, Chased Loss Got It Back Then Lost Everything Again," November 12, 2018. www.gamblingtherapy.org.

18. Quoted in Kate Wighton, "Gambling Addiction Triggers Same Brain Area as Alcohol and Drug Cravings," Neuroscience News, January 3, 2017. https://neurosciencenews.com.

19. Quoted in Terry J. Knapp, "Behaviorism and Public Policy: B.F. Skinner's Views on Gambling," *Behavior and Social Issues*, 1997. https://journals.uic.edu.

20. Jamie Madigan, "The Near Miss Effect and Game Rewards," Psychology of Games, September 2, 2016. www.psychologyofgames.com.

21. Hartney, "Signs of Pathological Gambling and Gambling Addiction."

Chapter Three: How Does Someone Become Addicted to Gambling?

22. Quoted in *Voices of Recovery* (blog), "The Ball," Lanie's Hope. http://lanieshope.org.

23. Quoted in Elizabeth Chuck, "For Compulsive Gamblers, Mega Millions Frenzy Means 'Constant Reminders to Play,'" NBC News, October 22, 2018. www.nbcnews.com.

24. Nealley, "Compulsive Gambling Is an Illness to Which I Lost Nearly Everything."

25. Nealley, "Compulsive Gambling Is an Illness to Which I Lost Nearly Everything."

26. Quoted in Peter Dizikes, "Understanding Gambling Addiction," MIT News, September 4, 2012. http://news.mit.edu.

27. Quoted in *Daily Telegraph* (London), "Children Shouldn't Play Games Like Candy Crush, Expert Warns," November 25, 2018. www.dailytelegraph.com.

28. Quoted in Daniel Bukszpan, "March Madness: These Successful People Nearly Lost It All to Gambling," *Fortune*, March 24, 2016. www.fortune.com.

29. Quoted in Alysse ElHage, "Breeding Addiction for Profit: The Social and Economic Harms of Casino Gambling," North Carolina Family, November 17, 2013. www.ncfamily.org.

30. Quoted in Rosengren, "How Casinos Enable Gambling Addicts."

Chapter Four: A Gambling Addict's Daily Struggle

31. Quoted in Laila Kearney, "As States Chase Sports Betting Gold, Addicts Left in the Cold," Reuters, October 26, 2018. www.reuters.com.

32. BoxingScene.com, "Compulsive Gamblers Struggle to Stop Gambling Even Though They Know They Have a Problem Gambling." www.boxingscene.com.

33. Quoted in Northstar Problem Gambling Alliance, "Attorneys at Increased Risk for Gambling Addiction," February 2, 2019. http://northstarproblemgambling.org.

34. Quoted in Northstar Problem Gambling Alliance, "Attorneys at Increased Risk for Gambling Addiction."

35. Quoted in Steve Foley, "Totally Consumed: Gambling Addiction Hurts—More than Just the Check Book," *Petoskey (MI) News-Review*, February 9, 2017. www.petoskeynews.com.
36. Quoted in Foley, "Totally Consumed."
37. Quoted in Foley, "Totally Consumed."
38. Quoted in Northstar Problem Gambling Alliance, "Real Voices: The Wife of a Problem Gambler Details Its Damaging Impact," December 5, 2012. http://northstarproblemgambling.org.
39. Quoted in Lanie's Hope, "Now I Have to Stop 'ITS KILLING Me.'" http://lanieshope.org.
40. Quoted in Kyle Schwab, "Admitted Gambling Addict Gets Prison for Embezzling $400K from OKC Company," News OK, June 9, 2018. www.newsok.com.
41. Quoted in Courtney Crowder and Kim Norvell, "After Lies, Embezzlement and $20,000 Bets, a Gambler Offers Remorse," *Des Moines (IA) Register*, June 27, 2018. www.desmoines register.com.

Chapter Five: Overcoming a Gambling Addiction

42. Quoted in Gambler ND, "Kirby's Story," 2019. www.gambler nd.com.
43. Quoted in John Riddle, "Gambling Addiction: Stats, Symptoms, and Treatment Options," PsyCom, January 8, 2019. www.psycom.net.
44. Gam-Anon, "Is a Gambling Problem Affecting Your Life?" www.gam-anon.org.
45. National Center for Responsible Gaming, "Brief Biosocial Gambling Screen," 2016. www.ncrg.org.
46. Quoted in Jonathan Wells, "How to Beat an Online Gambling Addiction," *Telegraph* (London), April 28, 2016. www .telegraph.co.uk.
47. Elizabeth Hartney, "Cognitive Behavioral Therapy for Addiction," Verywell Mind, October 14, 2017. www.verywellmind .com.

48. Quoted in 12Step.org, "12 Steps of Gamblers Anonymous." https://12step.org.

49. Casey, "Casey's Story," Gamtalk, August 23, 2017. www.gamtalk.org.

50. Debtfreeisthewaytobe, "A Solid Way to Beat That Gambling Urge MUST READ," Gambling Therapy, August 24, 2016. www.gamblingtherapy.org.

Evergreen Council on Problem Gambling
1821 Fourth Ave. E
Olympia, WA 98506
website: www.evergreencpg.org

The Evergreen Council on Problem Gambling is a nonprofit organization that provides services and programs for problem gamblers, their families, employers, students, treatment professionals, and the wider community. Their efforts include gambling addiction treatment support, advocacy, research, information, and education. Evergreen also has special programs for youth and underage gambling.

Gam-Anon International
PO Box 307
Massapequa Park, NY 11762
website: www.gam-anon.org

Gam-Anon is a twelve-step self-help fellowship of men and women who have been affected by the gambling problem of another. It seeks to help its members cope with frayed relationships, financial problems, and stress related to another person's gambling. Gam-Anon helps people find their way back to a normal way of thinking and living.

Gamblers Anonymous (GA)
PO Box 17173
Los Angeles, CA 90017
website: www.gamblersanonymous.org

GA is an organization dedicated to helping people recover from gambling addiction. Its members share their experience, strength, and hope with each other. The only requirement for membership is a desire to stop gambling. GA is supported by member contributions and does not require dues or fees.

Gambling Therapy: Online Help for Problem Gamblers
website: www.gamblingtherapy.org

Gambling Therapy is an online site that provides timely, expert, and up-to-date advice and support for problem gamblers and their dependents. It offers an intense level of support consisting of individual and group therapy.

Know the Odds
website: http://knowtheodds.org

Know the Odds seeks to raise awareness about problem gambling. It helps community members avoid gambling addiction and provides resources for those hurting from problem gambling. The website includes e-books, infographics, and videos with information about gambling addiction.

National Council on Problem Gambling (NCPG)
730 Eleventh St. NW, Suite 601
Washington, DC 20001
website: www.ncpgambling.org

The NCPG serves as the national advocate for programs and services to assist problem gamblers and their families. It also works to improve health and wellness by reducing the personal, social, and economic costs of problem gambling. The NCPG helps develop policies and programs for all those affected by problem gambling.

Books

Natasha Dow Schüll, *Addiction by Design: Machine Gambling in Las Vegas*. Princeton, NJ: Princeton University Press, 2014.

Sam Skolnik, *High Stakes: The Rising Cost of America's Gambling Addiction*. Boston: Beacon, 2015.

C.W.V. Straaten, *The Gambling Addiction Recovery Workbook*. True Potential Project, 2016.

Maia Szalavitz, *Unbroken Brain: A Revolutionary New Way of Understanding Addiction*. New York: Picador, 2016.

Arnie Wexler and Sheila Wexler, *All Bets Are Off: Losers, Liars, and Recovery from Gambling Addiction*. Las Vegas: Central Recovery, 2015.

Internet Sources

Daniel Bukszpan, "March Madness: These Successful People Nearly Lost It All to Gambling," *Fortune*, March 24, 2016. http://fortune.com.

Elizabeth Chuck, "For Compulsive Gamblers, Mega Millions Frenzy Means 'Constant Reminders to Play,'" NBC News, October 22, 2018. www.nbcnews.com.

CRC Health, "10 Myths of Compulsive Gambling." www.crchealth.com.

Tanya Mohn, "Fighting Compulsive Gambling Among Women," *New York Times*, April 28, 2017. www.nytimes.com.

Laura Parker, "Casinos Look to Video Games as a Draw for Millennials," *New York Times*, July 6, 2016. www.nytimes.com.

John Rosengren, "How Casinos Enable Gambling Addicts," *Atlantic*, December 2016. www.theatlantic.com.

Index

Picture Credits

Cover: mikkelwilliam/iStockphoto.com

 6: antonidiaz/Shutterstock.com

10: Ramon grosso dolarea/Shutterstock.com

13: Maury Aaseng

17: junpinzon/Shutterstock.com

22: Axel Bueckert/Shutterstock.com

25: Cliparea/Shutterstock.com

29: Boofoto/Shutterstock.com

34: Haizon/iStockphoto.com

36: monkeybusiness/Depositphotos

40: s_bukley/Shutterstock.com

46: Marcos Mesa Sam Wordley/Shutterstock.com

49: El Nartz/Shutterstock.com

52: wavebreakmedia/Shutterstock.com

57: pixelheadphoto/Shutterstock.com

60: Monkey Business Images/Shutterstock.com

64: ChameleonsEye/Shutterstock.com

John Allen is a writer who lives in Oklahoma City.